THEY ARE NC
THEY ARE F

Trilby Shaw

To my husband without whose help
and encouragement this would never have been written.

THEY ARE NOT LOST, THEY ARE HERE

Trilby Shaw

Published in the UK by:

Horizon Editions Limited,

trading as The Horizon Press, for the author.

Moor Farm Road West, Ashbourne, DE6 1HD

Tel: (01335) 347349

E-mail: books@thehorizonpress.co.uk

1st edition

ISBN: 978 184306 539 5

© Trilby Shaw 2011

The rights of Trilby Shaw as author of this work have been asserted by her in accordance with the Copyright, Design and Patents Act, 1988.
All rights reserved. No part of this publication may be reproduced, stored in a retrieval system or transmitted in any form or by any means, electronic, mechanical, photocopying, recording or otherwise without the prior permission of Horizon Editions Ltd.
British Library Cataloguing in Publication Data: a catalogue record for this book is available from the British Library.

Photographs

page 1: Soren Hawkes' drawing of ghost soldiers mustering at the Menin Gate
and realising that they are not forgotten
page 3: Trenches surviving at Sanctuary Wood Museum, near Hellfire Corner, Ypres

Front Cover: Menin Gate, Ypres
Back Cover left: Memorial Window, St John's Church, Ashbourne
Back Cover right: Memorial, St Oswald's Church, Ashbourne

Many of the images in this book are taken from local newspapers, which accounts for the poor quality.

FOREWORD

In 1961, the American iconic folk singers Pete Seeger and Joe Hickerson co-authored an evocative song about the war dead. You may recall the words of the final verse:

Where have all the graveyards gone?
Long time passing
Where have all the graveyards gone?
Long time ago
Where have all the graveyards gone?
Covered with flowers every one
When will we ever learn?
When will we ever learn?

We are always moved to sing these words in our mind as we reflect upon the waste of war. Without doubt, good or bad, the deaths of brave men and women change the history of us all. Trilby was well aware of the impact of these haunting words and they were an inspiration to her as she researched and wrote this book on the lives of the Ashbourne dead of World War I.

The author, Trilby Mary Mainwaring Shaw was born in Sheffield in 1938, the youngest of three children. She was evacuated at the age of three years to Ashbourne, where she attended the Church of England Junior School. From here, she progressed to the Queen Elizabeth Grammar School and then, at the age of thirteen, attended the Cavendish High School for Girls at Buxton. In 1957, Trilby married George Evelyn Shaw at St. Oswald's Church, Ashbourne and they celebrated their Golden Wedding in 2007 having lived their entire married life in Ashbourne. They had four children – twins Leonard and Margaret, Elizabeth and Richard. Trilby's enthusiasm for promoting the history, cultural and commercial development of Ashbourne is well acknowledged with her past membership of societies such as The Ashbourne Partnership, The Help Improve the Town Society, founder member of the Ashbourne Heritage Society and other organisations involved in the town's activities.

During the Napoleonic Prisoner of War Exhibition promoted by the Ashbourne Heritage Society in 1993, Trilby met and impressed Count Michael de Rochambeau, descendant of General Donatien Rochambeau who was incarcerated in Ashbourne during the Napoleonic Wars. Trilby was granted honorary membership of a branch of the French Foreign Legion by Count Rochambeau.

Trilby's dear, recently departed husband, George, wrote extensively about Ashbourne, particularly St. Oswald's Church. Sharing George's knowledge of Ashbourne and its people, Trilby assisted in editing her husband's work and is well qualified to take over George's mantle as an Ashbourne Historian. We are indebted to Trilby's effort in writing this well researched book. We in Ashbourne should never forget the sacrifices of our brave soldiers. To Trilby, they were not just names on a town cenotaph but real lives and her book pays a sincere tribute to each and every one. I have no hesitation in recommending this book. It is an important historical record.

Harry Wilson, President, Ashbourne Heritage Society

INTRODUCTION

Listening to the sermon on Remembrance Day 2007 about men who had no known grave, I was sad to think that the names on the Memorial were just that, names on a wall. Having been told by my mother and grandparents, the story of my uncle Pte. T. H. Mainwaring, I felt that other families had stories to tell. I feel extremely proud to have learned of the men who gave so freely their lives to make our country safe with bravery and courage which in normal times would never have surfaced. Ninety-five years on we can only imagine the mind set of these men, and I hope that after reading these humble researches you too will appreciate their sacrifice. I was advised to list names as on the memorial plaques, but I saw them as men who knew each other, possibly went to school together. I therefore have left them together as PALS and you will read of many who joined and died together. I have listed them according to burial places and have tried to give you a small history of each cemetery.

The figures given are hard to believe and put the sacrifices into perspective. Hopefully anyone who wishes to follow their own research will have a good starting point. I had only the Memorials to work on and you will find many errors. The memorial in St. Oswald's Church has more names than the War Memorial Gates. The Gates were erected by public subscription and the then Town Council, The War Graves Commission not coming into being for some years. The families were asked if they would like to have their loved ones commemorated. This was possible for a donation. Can you imagine a young widow with small children having to say NO I can't afford? How callous. Misspelling is common and one or two have been hard to trace e.g. Pte. J. Moon, Sherwood Foresters is correct whilst Pte J. Moon Lancashire Fusiliers should read Pte. J. Moore.

I have to thank a lot of people who have helped me with my research. My daughter Liz and her husband Brian, who have travelled "Flanders Fields" taking photographs and "Trench Tramping" through Belgium and the Somme. Without their help I could not have done it. Also thanks to Soren Hawkes MA a talented young artist living in Passchendaele who has given me permission to use his "*Ghost Soldiers at the Menin Gate*".

ACKNOWLEDGMENTS

Derbyshire County Council
Ashbourne Heritage Society
Sherwood Foresters Museum, Chilwell
Ashbourne Royal British Legion
Ashbourne News Telegraph Archives
B. B. C. News Service
Soren Hawkes M.A.
Ashbourne Antiques and Collectable Society

Trilby Shaw, Ashbourne, May 2011

IN FLANDERS FIELDS

In Flanders fields the poppies blow
Between the crosses, row on row,
That mark our place; and in the sky
The larks still bravely singing, fly
Scarce heard amid the guns below

We are the dead. Short days ago
We lived. Felt dawn, saw sunset glow,
Loved, and were loved, and now we lie
In Flanders Fields

Take up our quarrel with the foe:
To you with failing hands we throw
The torch, be yours to hold it high.
We shall not sleep, though poppies grow
In Flanders Fields

The poppy was chosen as the symbol of the Royal British Legion and became the most emotive symbol in the world. Why the poppy? It would seem to be appropriate after reading the above poem by Major John McCrae in 1915. But the poppy is not native to Europe. It was brought by the Mongol Emperor Genghis Khan when he invaded. The white opium poppy was brought from China and Afghanistan. Seeds were dropped and not seen again for many years. We hear of them again but the colour has changed, after the battle of Agincourt when the "field ran as red as blood, so profuse were the poppies."

The next time they are recorded was after Waterloo. It is thought that the Cavalry Charges and Artillery bombardments ploughed up the ground. The battles of the Great War again disturbed the ground and the poppies appeared again.

NOTES ON THE WAR MEMORIALS

ST OSWALD'S CHURCH

The memorial in St. Oswald's Church was unveiled in 1921 by Colonel G. D. Goodman CMG, DS0. 1t is made of Hopton Wood stone and is surmounted by the badge of the Notts. & Derbys Regiment. It was to be known later as the Sherwood Foresters, Worcester Foresters and is now the Mercian Regt. Ashbourne was one of their main recruiting towns.

The Memorial was designed by Lionel G. Pearson FRIBA. It is a simple plain stone tablet and the letters are picked out in scarlet.

Left: The War Memorial, St Oswald's Church, Ashbourne

Opposite top: The opening of the Memorial Gates in 1922

Opposite below: The Gates today

WAR MEMORIAL GATES

This is a more imposing monument. 1t is a massive construction made of Derbyshire Gritstone. Of late Doric design and extremely dignified, it forms the entrance to the Memorial Gardens and Recreation Ground. The opening is 12 feet wide, flanked by substantial buttresses, in the front of which stand two fluted columns 10 feet in height. Above the columns rises the pediment, enriched with suitable mouldings. The total height is over 15 feet. On the fascia over the gateway is carved a winged scarab, the sign of the Infinitive, with an endless knot the emblem of Perfect Love. Above are engraved the words "In Grateful Memory of Those Who Fell in the Great War". On the faces of the two buttresses are carved two Laurel wreaths, which give an appropriate canopy to the Bronze Panels containing the names of the fallen.

The whole of the work in connection with the Memorial Arch was executed by RG Lomas & Son, Monumental Masons, Derby. Through the gates the land is laid out as ornamental Gardens of Remembrance leading to a Recreation ground for the young of the town. The memorial was unveiled on Wednesday May 10th 1922 by the Rt. Hon. Baron Cullen of Ashbourne.

There are several other memorials in local churches to their members, but St. Johns on Buxton Road, as well as having commemorative panels, has a stained glass window given by the grieving families of the congregation. Unfortunately no record of the glazier is available.

THE GREEN HILLS OF ASHBOURNE

O dear to our hearts are the green hills of Ashbourne;
The breezes blow fresh over scenes that we love;
The flower-spangled meadows, the bird haunted wildwoods,
The rivulets wending their way to the Dove

But over these fair scenes the storm clouds are gathering,
Filling the air with war's dreadful alarms,
The signal rang out over hillside and valley –
"Your country doth need you, ye patriots. To arms"

Marching away o'er the green hills of Ashbourne,
Our brave lads were eager to answer the call;
With courage undaunted, they rushed to the conflict,
For King and for Country, to fight or to fall

In a land far away from the green hills of Ashbourne,
Our comrades were valiantly paying the debt;
For King and for Country they fought and they conquered;
O loyal and true hearts. We shall not forget.

They are gone for a while from the green hills of Ashbourne,
Their voices no more wake the echoes around;
The Last Post has spoken; the darkness has fallen;
Our soldiers will rest until the Reveille shall sound

Honour and love to the heroes who perished:
Honour and love to the patriot band;
On the green hills of Ashbourne their names will be cherished,
While those hills in their grandeur and beauty shall stand.

Lizzie Sinfield 1918

This poem was sent to His Majesty King George V and was accepted as a tribute to the men of Ashbourne who gave their lives.

Memorial Window, St John's Church

BELGIUM

CHESTER FARM CEMETERY

The cemetery contains 424 graves of Officers and Soldiers. It is named after the farmhouse that stood nearby.

Private A. Hollingshead

1437 1st/6th Sherwood Foresters
Died September 30 1915, aged 21

Son of Mr. & Mrs. F. Hollingshead of Dig Street, Ashbourne. He was killed in action when the Germans exploded a mine and shelled the trenches at Ouderdom. He had a brother Pte. F. Hollingshead, also serving in the same battalion who was awarded the Military Medal for "Carrying ammunition to the Front under fire."

COXYDE MILITARY CEMETERY

Contains 1,517 graves of Officers and Soldiers. The cemetery was enlarged after the Armistice and took in several small cemeteries.

Bombardier Walter Burton

89865 D. Battery 51st. Brigade Royal Field Artillery
Died November 13 1917, aged 26

Son of Mr. & Mrs. William Burton, Ashbourne. He had worked at Tissington Hall since leaving school and had 3 brothers serving. Driver Wm. Burton, Army Service Corps., Pte. Fred Burton, Lincolnshire Regt. and Pte. Jack Burton, Lancashire Territorials.

"They shall grow not old as we that are left grow old:
Age shall not weary them, nor the years condemn.
At the going down of the sun and in the morning
We will remember them."

~ Laurence Binyon

The Menin Gate

DOZINGHEM MILITARY CEMETERY

Contains 3,239 graves of Officers and Soldiers. The cemetery was close to 3 clearing stations until 1918. 1t also contains many World War II graves.

Private A. Silvester

116540 104th Company Machine Gun Corps (Infantry)
Died November 23 1917, aged 26

Son of William H. Silvester, Woodbine Cottage, Derby Road, Ashbourne. He had a brother Pte. A. Silvester serving with the Kings Own Yorkshire Light Infantry in France.

DUHALLOW A.D.S. CEMETERY

The cemetery contains 1,601 graves of Officers and Soldiers. Fifty-four of these are German. A.D.S. stands for Advanced Dressing Station. The name Duhallow is after a Southern Irish hunt.

Corporal C. Mellor

20897/18th. Btn. Lancashire Fusiliers
Died October 15 1918

KEMMEL CHATEAU MILTARY CEMETERY

Kemmel Chateau Military Cemetery contains the graves of 1,135 Officers and Soldiers.

Lance Corporal Alec Ford

Landed in France 28 February 1915
1349 1st/6th Sherwood Foresters
Died May 26 1915, aged 23

Son of Mary Plowman (formerly Ford), Spencers Yard, St. John St. He was killed in action in the trenches at Kemmel. He had a stepbrother serving with the Royal Scots at Passchendaele.

Lance Corporal Albert H. Harrison

Landed in France 28 February 1915
1814 1/6th Sherwood Foresters
Died April 9 1915, aged 19

Son of Harry & Emily Harrison, Devon House, Mayfield Road. His father was the Manager of the Ashbourne Gas Works at the time. He was killed in action by German shellfire in the trenches at Kemmel.

Pte. Walter Blake

Landed in France 28 February 1915
1592 1/6th Sherwood Foresters
Died April 9 1915, aged 22

Son of Walter & Lucy Blake, Union Street Ashbourne. He had been a member of Territorial Army since 1911. He had two brothers serving at the time in the same Btn., Pte. Sydney Blake and Pte. Albert Victor Blake; both returned.

Pte. Walter Blake

Pte. Frederick J Bull

Landed in France February 28 1915
1457 1/6th Sherwood Foresters
Died April 9 1915, aged 26

Son of Harry & Annie Bull, Compton, Ashbourne. Killed by a German shell whilst serving in the trenches at Kemmel.

The last three named are an example of three men joining up together and dying together.

LA CLYTTE MILITARY CEMETERY

La Clytte was used as Brigade Headquarters. 1,082 graves are located here, 1,010 are British.

44756 Bombardier D. Hepworth

103rd. A Battery Royal Field Artillery
Died October 21 1917, aged 24

His family added to the headstone a private tribute:

'May the Heavenly Winds
Blow softly o'er
This sweet and hallowed spot'

LIJSSENTHOEK MILITARY CEMETERY

Lijssenthoek is the second largest Commonwealth cemetery in Belgium. It contains 9,901 burials and 883 war graves of other nationalities.

Lance Corporal Leonard Thorpe

22912 6 Btn. Kings Own Scottish Borderers
Died October 4 1918, aged 35

LINDENHOEK CHALET MILITARY CEMETERY

Lindenhoek cemetery contains 315 graves of Officers and Soldiers.

Pte. John Gladstone Woodyatt

2479 1/5th. Sherwood Foresters
Died April 28 1915, aged 28

Son of J.H. Pitt Woodyatt & Constance Woodyatt of Compton
and husband of Kate Woodyatt of Kirk Langley. Killed in action
by a rifle bullet in the trenches at Lindenhoek whilst acting as
signaller. He was originally buried in a private garden at Hill
60 and re-interred later. He is remembered on the memorial
in Trinity Methodist Church, Ashbourne.

MENDINGHEM MILITARY CEMETERY

Mendinghem contains 2,442 graves Officers and Soldiers, 2,300 of these are British.
Mendinghem is one of a trio of cemeteries given names by the troops to recognise the
work of the Casualty Clearing Stations stationed there; the other two are Badaghem and
Dozinghem.

Lance Corporal F. W. Wallis

21172 3rd. Btn Grenadier Guards
Died September 13 1917, aged 23

Son of Robert & Eva Wallis, Mayfield Road.
  In the memorial service at All Saints Catholic Church L/Cpl. Wallis was remembered as a
regular worshipper who was "a lad with all the prospects of a happy life before him, full of
health and strength. His country spoke to him in the name of God, and he did not hesitate
to say – I must do my bit to defend my home and my dear ones. And he went. He was
wounded, and when he was recovered went back willingly and not in ignorance of what
that meant. He paid the supreme sacrifice." He was grandson of Mrs. Fanny Wallis of the
Green Man Hotel.

Pte. A. Mellor

35878 4th. Btn North Staffordshire Regt.
Died December 2 1917

THE MENIN GATE
MEMORIAL TO THE MISSING: YPRES

The Menin Gate Memorial commemorates Officers and Soldiers of the British Expeditionary Force who died on the Ypres Salient, known as Flanders Fields. They are remembered every night at 8.00pm with the Last Post Ceremony. This was started on July 1st 1928 for a short period and then daily from November 11th 1929. The only exception to this has been from May 20th 1940 to September 6th 1944 during the four years of German occupation in World War II. The end panel of the Gate has the inscription:

TO THE ARMIES

OF THE BRITISH EMPIRE

WHO STOOD HERE

FROM 1914 – 1918

AND TO THOSE OF THEIR DEAD

WHO HAVE NO KNOWN GRAVE

Sergeant W. A. Wibberley

144 1/6th. Bn. Sherwood Foresters
Died September 30 1915
Son of Mr. & Mrs. W H Wibberley, Ashbourne.
Killed in action when the Germans exploded a
mine and shelled the trenches at Ouderdon.

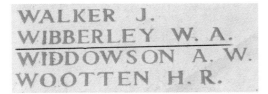

WALKER J.
WIBBERLEY W. A.
WIDDOWSON A. W.
WOOTTEN H. R.

Lance Corporal George Bailey

1400 1/6th. Bn. Sherwood Foresters
Died September 10 1917, aged 21

Son of Mr. & Mrs. Bailey St. John Street,
Ashbourne.
Wounded on 3-5-1915 at Kemmel.
Wounded on 7-6-1915 at Kemmel.
Killed in action when serving near Fouquiere,
in the Cambrin sector.

LANCE CORPORAL
ALLEN T.
BAILEY G.
BAINES C.
BURGESS H.

Lance Corporal Arthur Harding

1953 1/6th Bn. Sherwood Foresters
Died September 30 1915, aged 21

Son of James & Alice Harding, Compton, Ashbourne. Member of the church choir St. Oswald's Church, Ashbourne. Prior to war service he was employed by Ashbourne News Office. Killed in action when the Germans exploded a mine and shelled the trenches near Ouderdon. He had a brother serving in Iraq.

Rifleman Frank Atkins

Z/1306 2nd Bn. Rifle Brigade
Died July 13 1917

ASPLAND J. R.
ATHERTON T. H
ATKINS F.
ATKINS J. S.

Pte. Claude Boden

81367 56th Field Ambulance, RAMC
Died July 31 1917, aged 20

Son of Mrs. Boden, Green Road, Ashbourne. Killed when struck by a piece of shell whilst helping the wounded. He was amongst those who received the first batch of wounded at the local Red Cross Hospital, March 1915. He had a brother serving with the Transport Corps., in East Africa. He was employed in the printing room at the Ashbourne Telegraph.

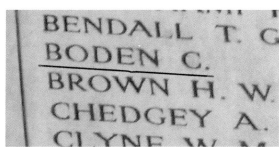

BENDALL T. G
BODEN C.
BROWN H. W.
CHEDGEY A.
CLYNE W. M

Pte. Charles Carter

2524 1/6th Bn. Sherwood Foresters
Died September 30 1915, aged 19

Son of Edward & Martha Carter, Market Place, Ashbourne. His twin brother Thomas was also killed in action.

Pte. F. W. Cox

36193 16th Bn. Sherwood Foresters
Died July 31 1917

Pte. Charles Carter

Pte. F. W. Cox

Pte. J. Perry

13818 10th. Bn. Sherwood Foresters
Died December 14, aged 25

Son of Mary Ann Allan, Stone House, Ashbourne.

Pte. A. Roberts

3561 1/6th. Bn. Sherwood Foresters
Died September 30 1915

Son of Joseph & Harriet Roberts. Killed in action when the Germans exploded a mine and shelled the trenches at Ouderdon.

Pte. A. Roberts

Pte. B.A. Ward

17308 10th Bn. Sherwood Foresters
Died February 14 1916, aged 21

Son of John & Susannah Frances Ward. Reported missing February 2nd 1916. Killed in action during a German raid near the canal south-east of Ypres.

Pte. Charles Ward

S/11370 8th. Bn. Seaforth Highlanders
Died August 2 1917, aged 23

Son of Frank & Fanny Ward, Harvey House, Green Road, Ashbourne. When the regiment was advancing he was hit by a shell and died instantly. A church goer, he had received communion the day he died.

Pte. O. E. Slater RVM

13466 lst. Bn. Grenadier Guards
Died October 30 1914, aged 25

PRIVATE OWEN EDMUND SLATER
1st Batt. Grenadier Guards.

Son of Mr. & Mrs. W. Slater, 91 Mayfield Road. Husband of Caroline Edith Slater, 42 Millgreen Road, Hayward Heath.

Pte. Slater was an enigma which needed solving. He is remembered on the Church Memorial and also the Memorial Gates. This is normal, but another memorial to Slater is in the South transept of St. Oswald's Church. A simple white marble slab erected by his Officer "In memory of a faithful servant." What had this local man done to receive this honour? The Royal Victoria Medal is not a military medal, but a gift of the Monarch for personal services to the Monarch. I therefore had to contact the Royal Archives. Buckingham Palace could not help but put me on to the Round Tower at Windsor Castle.

Their records show that Guardsman Slater was awarded the medal on June 7 1910 for his services at the funeral of King Edward VII. He was a member of the King's Company that provided the bearer party to carry and escort the coffin. At the time he would have been 20 years of age. 1914 sees him as an Officer's valet (batman) living at 37 Somerset Buildings, Belgrave Square, London where he met and married Caroline, also in service. He was killed 3 months later.

He landed with his Officer on October 7 1914. The 1st Grenadier Guards had arrived at Southampton two days previously – crossing in two vessels *SS Armenian* and *SS Turcoman*. The latter being called by Rt. Hon. Sir Frederick Ponsonby in his war history as 'Just a cattle boat." Two train journeys later the Grenadiers were at Ghent on October 9th, where, from a local dye-works, the Belgian authorities issued large rolls of velvet in lieu of blankets. The Ulahns – German infantry – were sighted on October 14th and the Battalion suffered many casualties. A lot were buried alive under as much as three feet of earth.

A letter to Mr. W. Slater from Slater's Officer states that, "I was taken ill at the Front and could not move from where I was. Owen stayed with me and carried me through a hail of bullets and artillery fire and brought me safely to hospital. He returned to the Front and died." Lt. Symons erected memorials to Owen Slater not only in Ashbourne but also in Much Dewchurch, Hereford where his family owned the estate. Guardsman Slater had a brother Pte. H.G. Slater serving in France.

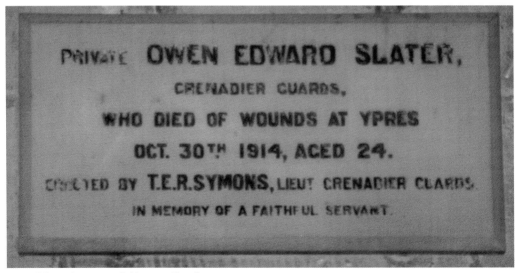

Memorial, south transept, Ashbourne Church

Pte. James Wardle

3550 1/6th. Bn. Sherwood Foresters
Died September 30 1915, aged 17

Son of Mrs. Wardle, The Channel, Ashbourne. Landed in France June 28th 1915. Killed in action when the Germans exploded a mine and shelled the trenches near Ouderdon.

In this one incident, eight local boys died together in the same action.

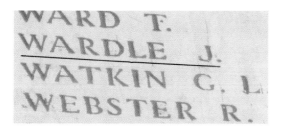

Pte. H. Wibberley

58721 11th. Bn. Sherwood Foresters
Died June 7 1917

Killed in action when in the attack near Hill 60.

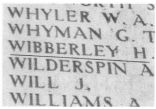

NO MANS COT CEMETRY

No Mans Cot contains 79 British Officers and Soldiers. This cemetery is named after a building which stood on the south side of Admirals Road in between Boezinge and Wielte.

Pte. P French

9521 6th. Bn. East Yorkshire Regt.
Died July 17 1917

Son of Mr. & Mrs. French, Spencers Yard, St. John Street.

PLOEGSTEERT MEMORIAL

The Ploegsteert Memorial commemorates 11,000 British and South African soldiers who died in this sector and have no known grave. Soldiers not able to pronounce the name called it "PLUGSTREET."

Pte. G. L. Osborn

141328 25th. Bn. Machine Gun Corps (Infantry)
Died April 10 1918, aged 19

Son of Esther Osborn and the late George Osborn, 32 Mayfield Road.

Pte. F. Wint

106268 2/6th Sherwood Foresters
Died April 18 1918, aged 19

Son of James & Sarah Wint, 30 Mayfield Road. Reported missing April 18 1918. Killed April 19 1918 whilst serving in the trenches at Kemmel. Brother of Pte. A. Wint, also of the 2/6th, survived. Related to Cpl. A.E. Wint who was mentioned in despatches and died of wounds April 18th 1918.

NEW IRISH FARM CEMETERY

New Irish farm contains 4,716 Officers and Soldiers. Named after a farm that stood nearby until 1917. At the Armistice the cemetery contained only 73 burials in 3 irregular rows. After the War it became a relocation cemetery, and bodies of the dead were brought here from roadside graves, surrounding battlefields and small isolated cemeteries.

Pte. T. H. Mainwaring

240611 2/6th Bn. Sherwood Foresters
Died September 27 1917, aged 20

The son of William & Sarah Mainwaring, Buxton Road.

Employed by local corset makers Richard Cooper, as a guillotine cutter. He was a member of Ashbourne Town Band, playing the cornet. He was also a keen Scout and was Company Bugler. One night in November 1914, he together with 4 other boys marched from a Scout meeting to the Town Hall. Dr. Hollick Snr. in three hours that night passed as fit for duty 95 men and boys. The Scouts were included. This was to be the nucleus of the 2/6th. Battalion. They marched to Buxton and were billeted at the Empire Hotel. Harry was promoted to Company Bugler, but within hours he realised that the bugle issued by the Army was no good. He got permission from his Commanding Officer to send for his own bugle and this was used until his death in Belgium.

Within days they were sent to the Cat and Fiddle Inn on the Derbyshire Moors in the charge of a Sergeant and given a uniform and a rifle. They had no formal training. Eventually they were sent by a circuitous route around the coast of Ireland to Dublin. As they had only rudimentary training they were nicknamed "Wild men of the Peak" and on landing in Ireland, prior to the Easter Rising, they fought their first battle at Ashbourne outside Dublin. Taking part in the Rising and showing great bravery they were eventually shipped to Belgium where they were broken up amongst the Brigade to act as Runners, a very dangerous occupation.

In 1916 he was wounded in the arm and caught Dysentery. He returned to his unit and saw service on the Ypres Salient. He was known to have taken Communion with his father on the day of his death. His father being too old for combat service and having been a regular soldier previously serving in Afghanistan was serving in a Labour Corps on the Salient at the time. On the day before his death he jumped into a trench and trod on something hard. On investigation it proved to be a German bugle. He picked it up and put it into his knapsack. The morning of his death he was again wounded and lay on a stretcher at the side of the road. The first vehicle to pass was an ambulance driven by an Ashbourne man, in fact a cousin, Pte. L. Avery.

He stopped to speak and promised that he would come back for Harry. On returning, the 5 stretchers in a row had been machine gunned by German planes and all were dead. His belongings were returned to the family, including the German bugle. Both bugles remained with the family, Harry's own bugle being played at every Remembrance Day service until the 1950s when the Town Band took over. Both bugles were united in 2004 and are now in the Foresters Museum. His Officer, writing to the family, said "I have known your son since he joined us at Buxton as a little bugler. I have watched him grow up, and became very fond of him. He had been selected as a runner for the Brigade, and met his death whilst engaged in this important duty." He was killed at Vlamertinge and was previously buried at Zonnebeke.

The 2/6th Battalion was only in existence for the duration of the War, being raised for Ireland. This is an example of mistakes on Memorials. St. Oswald's reads Pte G H Mainwaring. Town memorial reads Pte T H Mainwaring which is correct.

PRISCHES COMMUNAL CEMETERY

Prisches Communal Cemetery contains the graves of 3 soldiers of the Great War. Of the 3 casualties here, one is from the very beginning of the War – August 1914. The other 2 are from the very end – close to Armistice 1918.

Lance Corporal Caleb E. Tanner DCM MM

241535 /6th Btn. Sherwood Foresters
Died November 5 1918, aged 21

Son of Arthur and Sarah Tanner, King Street. He was one of the youngsters who joined up in the early days of the War, being barely old enough. He displayed outstanding bravery on at least two occasions for which he was decorated. He must have been one of the exceptional characters that war throws up. He came from an unexceptional family but

showed unimaginable bravery. His name is now forgotten. His Gazette notices read:

London Gazette 12/3/1919

"Distinguished Conduct Medal. For splendid gallantry and initiative near Montrebehain on 3rd October 1918. After taking the surrender of 30 prisoners single handed, he went on and personally captured a machine gun killing all the team himself. When the enemy were evacuating the village, seeing some gun limbers limbering up to withdraw, he succeeded in wiping out both horses and men with his Lewis gun. Seeing the right flank being held up by machine gun fire, he gave covering fire of his own initiative, thus allowing his comrades to advance. Throughout the whole operation he showed absolute disregard for danger and the greatest initiative."

This alone should have gained him a place in history, but on a later date he was awarded a further award:

London Gazette 14/5/1919

"Military Medal. For courage and fighting spirit during the attack on Bellenglise and Lehaucourt on 29th September 1918. This man alone took 2 Officers and 30 prisoners. He also did exceptionally good work throughout the whole attack with his Lewis gun."

However this was not the end of the story.

The story of his last day was related during my research by the grandson of Pte. F. Hollinshead MM.

"Basically what happened that day was that 2 soldiers had gone into no-man's land to repair a telephone line at the listening post and as they went out a Germen sniper shot them both. One was killed instantly and the other was alive and moving. Tanner said "I am going to fetch him in Frank because he is somebody's son." Hollinshead replied that he would be killed because they could not see the sniper. Tanner said he was going, and crept to get to the wounded soldier. He started to drag him back but the German shot Tanner through the head. Hollinshead saw the puff of smoke from the snipers gun and pinpointed his position. He shot into the trees with his Lewis gun killing the sniper. The man who went to fetch Tanner in was another local man Jack Poyser who was also awarded the MM. Tanner was put in for the Victoria Cross, but when it was put before the Commanding Officer he said that Tanner *"was mad to have gone out there."* No further action was taken.

TOURNAI COMMUNAL CEMETRY, ALLIED DIVISION

Tournai contains 808 graves. After the Armistice a casualty clearing station was set up here.

Driver J.W. Gallimore

T/382629 1st Company 741 Div. Train, Royal Army Service Corps. Formerly 6th Battalion Sherwood Foresters.
Died December 27 1918, aged 21

Son of Thomas and the late Lucy Gallimore, Buxton Road. Enlisted in Notts and Derbys, later transferred to Royal Army Service Corps.

TYNE COT MEMORIAL AND CEMETERY

Tyne Cot is the largest Commonwealth cemetery in the world. It is also the most important reminder of the bloody battle of Passchendaele. During the British offensive of 1917 tens of thousands of soldiers died here in a period of 100 days for a gain of barely 8 kilometres (5 miles). Originally Tyne Cot was a bunker on the German Flandern 1 line. On October 4th 1917, Australian soldiers captured the position and used it as an Advanced Dressing Station. 300 Soldiers died here and were buried. Between 1919 and 1921, specialist units called Exhumation Companies brought 12,000 to Tyne Cot from surrounding sites. Most of them have no known name (being unrecognisable). The rear wall of the cemetery is a Memorial to the Missing. 1t bears the names of 35,000 British and New Zealand servicemen who died in 1917. The Tyne Cot Memorial also continues the surplus 35,000 from the Menin Gate. Every year over 180,000 visitors from all over the world come to pay homage.

Lance Corporal F.T. French

36128 7th Btn. Leicestershire Regiment
Died October 30 1917, aged 29

Son of Mr. & Mrs. French, South Street. Husband of Mary French, (née Newton). He left a 16 month old child.

He landed in France December 16 1916 and was wounded slightly on three occasions. He was in charge of a Lewis gun team and has no known grave.

Pte. J.C. Taylor

18545 9th Btn Sherwood Foresters
Died August 19 1917, aged 26

Son of Mr. & Mrs. Tom and Grace Taylor, Dig Street.

John Clifford Taylor is the only Ashbourne man to have a registered grave in Tyne Cot cemetery. He enlisted in 1915 and after training was sent to Gallipoli. He later went to Egypt, Italy and then on to France. He was killed in action whilst serving in the trenches near Steenbeke.

Prior to war service he worked at Howell and Marsden (grocers in St John Street). He was one of 4 brothers who served in the war. Wilfred served with the Royal Army Medical Corps. He had started work as office boy at Holland Rigby and Williams, solicitors. He returned after the war and served for 30 years with the firm. Ashbourne Petty Sessions recorded him "*extremely able as Clerk.*" He lived at Leys House, Station Street. Brother Ernest was Corporal in the Grenadier Guards and was later transferred to 2nd Sussex Regt. After the war he served in India from 1921; he returned. The youngest son Reginald was killed on September 9 1918 aged 21 and is buried at Westoutre.

Pte. W Blood

268841 16th Btn Sherwood Foresters
Died November 5 1917. He has no known grave.

Pte. Enoch Bull

36209 7th Btn Leicestershire Regiment
Died October 9 1917, aged 30

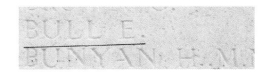

Son of the late Enoch & Elizabeth Bull of Kirk Langley, he married Mary Louisa Thacker of Sturston Road. He has no known grave. His name is not on the Ashbourne Memorials, but is on a grave in the Churchyard.

Pte J.W. Locker

81300 15th Btn. Durham Light Infantry
Died April 27 1918, aged 18

Son of Mr. & Mrs. John W. and Violet Ann Locker, Buxton Road.
   The death of her son turned Mrs. Locker's mind and for the rest of her life had to undergo treatment.

Pte J. Hellaby

70706 1st Btn. Sherwood Foresters
Died July 7 1917, aged 35

Son of Mr. & Mrs. J.H. Hellaby Old Hall Farm, Yeldersley. Husband of Annie Hellaby, Upper Mayfield. He enlisted in the 2/6th Btn Sherwood Foresters in October 1914 and served in the Easter Rising, Dublin. He was transferred to 1st Btn in September 1916. Wounded on October 30 1916, he returned to duty on December 28 1916. He was injured again on April 4 1917 and returned to duty on April 24 1917. He was killed in action by German shellfire when serving in the trenches at the Menin Gate near Ypres.

VLAMERTINGE NEW CEMETERY

Pte G. W. Plowman

201990 1/8th Btn. Royal Scots Regiment
Died September 24 1917, aged 19

Son of Mr. George W. Plowman & Mrs. Mary
Plowman of Ashbourne. Step brother of L/
Cpl A. Ford killed at Kemmel.

WESTOUTRE BRITISH CEMETERY

Westoutre contains the graves of 175 Officers and Soldiers – 167 British.

Sergeant R Taylor

241126 2/6th Btn Sherwood Foresters
Died September 26 1917, aged 21

Son of Tom & Grace Taylor, Dig Street. Husband of Mrs. W Taylor 35 Violet Street, Derby.
He enlisted October 1914 and served in the Easter Rising, Dublin before going to Belgium.
He was killed in action when in the attack near Vlamertinghe. Brother J. C. Taylor is buried
at Tyne Cot.

WULVERGHEM-LINDENHOEK RD.
MILITARY CEMETERY

Wulverghem – Lindenhoek Road has 1,010 burials, 843 of them British. The cemetery was
first known as Wulverghem Dressing Station Cemetery. It was used from 1914 to 1917 and
at the end of the war had just 163 graves. It was later much enlarged with burials brought
from the battlefields.

Pte T. Hudson

G/7439 3rd. Btn Middlesex Regiment
Died July 24 1915. Died of wounds

YPRES TOWN CEMETERY

Ypres town cemetery has 598 graves of Officers and Soldiers, 568 of these are British. As the name suggests, the cemetery is in the town close to the Menin Gate. A number of graves are to soldiers of World War II.

Gunner W. Thacker

366215 301st Siege Battery, Royal Garrison Artillery
Died July 31 1917, aged 37

He was the eldest son of Mr. and Mrs. W Thacker of Sturston Road and husband of Frances Thacker, also of Sturston Road, who had one child. He enlisted as a war-time volunteer who joined as a Territorial soldier in the North Scottish Royal Garrison Artillery Territorial Force. Training in Scotland and at Lydd, Kent, he was transferred to 301st Siege Battery Royal Garrison Artillery and was sent to France and Flanders in 1916/17. He was killed when his Siege Battery was laying down barrage fire during the opening stage of the Third Battle of Ypres (Passchendaele) on July 31st 1917. He is buried in the cemetery extension. He had a brother George Thacker serving in the Sherwood Foresters at the time and a brother-in law Enoch Bull, also in the Sherwood Foresters, who was killed and is on the Tyne Cot Memorial.

ZANTVOORDE BRITISH CEMETERY

Zantvoorde contains the graves of 1,583 Officers and Soldiers. The village of Zantvoorde near Ypres was lost to the Germans on October 30th 1914 and remained in enemy hands until it was finally retaken on September 28th 1918.

Lance Corporal Clifford Kitchen

59446 15th Btn. Sherwood Foresters
Died October 1 1918 aged 31

Son of Thomas and Rose Annie Kitchen of Ashbourne, husband of Sarah Ann Kitchen. He was connected with the VAD (Voluntary Aid Detachment) hospital in Ashbourne for a long time, prior to enlisting. His brother Sapper Harry Kitchen was killed and buried at Pieta Military Cemetery, Malta.

FRANCE

ABBEVILLE COMMUNAL CEMETERY

Abbeville contains 774 graves of British and Commonwealth Soldiers.

Corporal R. H. Salt

27865 1st Army Corps H.Q. Signal Company Royal Engineers
Died November 18 1914, aged 20

Son of Israel & Emily Salt, Mayfield Road. Died of wounds.

ABBEVILLE COMMUNAL CEMETERY EXTENSION

Attached to the Abbeville cemetery the extension contains 1,754 graves of the Great War, of these 1,376 are British.

A. I. F. BURIAL GROUND, FLERS

A. I. F. Burial Ground contains 3,580 graves of Officers and Soldiers, 2,815 are British.

Pte. J. Brown

70773 lst Btn Sherwood Foresters
Died October 26 1916

Son of Mr. & Mrs. G Brown of Union Street. He was married with a wife living with parents. Killed in action when serving in the trenches near Trones Wood on the Somme.

ARRAS MEMORIAL

Arras Memorial commemorates 34,717 British, South African and New Zealand Officers and Soldiers. It stands in the Fauborg D'Amiens Cemetery.

Rifleman F. Allen

YM84 2nd Btn Kings Royal Rifle Corps

Born in Ashbourne but living in Derby. Commemorated on the St. Oswald's Memorial.

Pte. C. V. Belfield

41947 3rd Btn Worcestershire Regt.
Died March 22 1918

Pte. F. Courtman

25446 10th Prince of Wales Own Hussars
Died April 11 1917

Pte John Nelson Ginever

204399 2/4th Btn York and Lancaster Regiment
Died May 3 1917, aged 21

Son of Mr. John Nelson & Harriet Ginever of Station Street. Born at Rampton, Notts., he worked as a coal delivery man before joining the army. He left 2 brothers and 4 sisters.

Pte. Charles Sowter

2161 8th. Btn Lincolnshire Regiment
Died April 28 1917, aged 24

Third son of Mr. & Mrs. James Sowter, Old Derby Road. His wife was living in Mayfield. Formerly employed by Mr. G. Gaunt, a builder, and was married just before leaving England. His brother, Pte. Fred Sowter of the Sherwood Foresters had been a prisoner of war in Germany for some time.

AVELUY WOOD CEMETERY

Aveluy Wood, also known as the Lancashire Dump, has 380 graves, 354 are British. It is only 3 miles/5km north of Albert, the centre of the Somme Battlefields.

Pte Timothy Blood

70732 Btn. Sherwood Foresters
Died March 4 1917, aged 35

Son of Charles & Alice Blood of Mayfield and husband of Hannah Elizabeth of King Street. Killed in action during the attack on Andover, France.

BAGNEUS BRITISH CEMETERY, GEZAINCOURT

Bagneus Cemetery at Gezaincourt has 1,374 graves. 1,145 of these are British.

Pte. F. Blood

83231 2/8th Btn Sherwood Foresters, transferred to 101st Labour Corps with new number 476346
Died May 20 1918, aged 38

Son of John & Mary Blood of Ashbourne. Husband of Mary Blood of Station Street. Died of wounds whilst serving with the Service Corps.

CAMBRAI MEMORIAL, LOUVERAL

The Cambrai Memorial commemorates 7,041 Officers and Soldiers who died in November and December 1917 at the battle of Cambrai. They have no known graves.

Sergeant H. Avery

24117 2/6th Sherwood Foresters
Died December 1 1917, aged 20

Son of Mr. & Mrs. Avery, Station Street. Enlisted September 1914 aged 17 and trained at Buxton. Was 1st Class Musketry Sergeant before his 19th birthday and served in the Irish Rebellion in 1916. Killed in action by shrapnel from a shell during the attack near Vacquerie.

Pte W. Twigge

240601 2/6th Sherwood Foresters
Died December 1 1917, aged 36

Son of Joseph & Fanny Twigge of Peter Street. Husband of Ada Twigge, Wyaston Road.
   Killed in action near Vacquerie.

CITE BONJEAN MILITARY CEMETERY

Cite Bonjean Military Cemetery contains the graves of 2,604 Officers and Soldiers, 1,190 of them are British, 472 are German. Armentieres was within the Allied lines from October 17 1914 until the German advance of 1918. 1t was not retaken by the Allies until October 1918. 1n 1925, 455 German graves were removed but almost 500 still remain.

Pte. J. Chell

11214 7th Btn Lincolnshire Regiment
Died March 25 1917

Killed in action.

COJEUL BRITISH CEMETERY

Cojeul contains 397 British graves.

Pte. Albert Silvester MM

12/506 9th Btn. Kings Own Yorkshire Light Infantry
Died April 9 1917, aged 32

Son of William H. Silvester, Woodbine Cottage, Ashbourne. Husband of May Silvester, Pontefract, Yorks. Brother of Pte. A. Silvester buried at Dozinghem.

DELSAUX FARM CEMETERY

Delsaux Farm Cemetery contains 495 graves of Officers and Soldiers.

Pte. W.H.J. Phipps

235319 2nd Btn Suffolk Regiment
Died October 9, 1918

Son of Charles & Catherine Phipps of The Grammar School, Ashbourne. It is presumed that Mr. Phipps was Housemaster.

ECOIVRES MILITARY CEMETERY, MONT-ST ELOI

Ecoivres Military Cemetery contains 2,515 graves including 787 French and 4 German.

Pte. A. Housley

3548 6th Btn Sherwood Foresters
Died April 3 1916, aged 20

Son of Thomas & Sarah Ann Housley of Ashbourne. Enlisted when 19, he worked previously at Hunters Stores, Dig Street. Was killed by a sniper when serving in the trenches at Acq.

Pte L. Twigg

3568 6th Btn Sherwood Foresters
Died April 10 1916, aged 21

Son of Henry Alsop Twigge, 14 The Leys, Ashbourne.

Pte. A. Housley   Pte L. Twigg

ERQUINGHEM- LYS CHURCHYARD EXTENSION

Erquinghem-Lys Churchyard Extension contains the graves of 600 Officers and Soldiers, 522 of them are British.

Pte. H. Walton

7965 1st Btn Staffordshire Regiment
Died October 23 1914

ESTAIRES COMMUNAL CEMETERY and EXTENSION

Estaires Communal Cemetery and Extension contains 918 graves of the Great War. Of these 665 are British. Estaires town was occupied by French cavalry on October 15 1914 and passed immediately into British hands.

Pte W. King

A/2300 12th Btn Kings Royal Rifle Corps
Died September 25 1915, aged 19

Son of Mrs. Louise King. Born in Ashbourne. Died of wounds.

ETAPLES MILITARY CEMETERY

Etaples military cemetery contains the graves of 10,770 British and Commonwealth Officers and Soldiers. During the Great War the area around Etaples was the scene of immense concentration of Commonwealth reinforcements camps and hospitals. It was remote from attack except by air and easily accessible by rail from both Northern and Southern battlefields. In 1917, 10,000 troops were camped amongst the sand dunes and the hospitals. The hospitals included 11 General 1 Stationary, 4 Red Cross and 1 convalescent depot, which could deal with 22,000 sick and wounded. It was 27km from Boulogne.

Etaples Military Cemetery

Lance Sergeant H. M. Webster

11238 Grenadier Guards
Died December 8 1917

Relation to Webster the Dairyman, Compton.
Possibly a grandson brought up by Mr. Webster
Snr. Died of wounds.

Pte. H. Courtman

10235 213th Coy. Machine Gun Corps.
Died July 28 1917
Probably brother of Trooper F. Courtman killed April 11 1917, Arras.

Pte E. Plant

241601 2/7th Sherwood Foresters
Died May 7 1918, aged 38

Son of the late William & Eliza Plant of Ashbourne.
Nephew of Mr. J. Plant, Union Street, Chemist. Had
previously been wounded (not recorded). Admitted
to hospital on April 17 1918 suffering from gunshot
wounds to the head and severe wounds to the left leg.
Died of wounds at 22nd General Hospital, Carnieres.

Gunner F. W. Potter

73629 146th Siege Battery, Royal Garrison Artillery
Died April 7 1918, aged 22

Son of Robert James & Annie Potter. Probably Potters
Corn Merchant.

FINS NEW BRITISH CEMETERY, SOMME

Fins New British Cemetery contains 1,523 graves of the Great War. Of these 1,193 are
British. Fins is a village lying between Cambrai and Peronne. There are also 233 German
burials here.

Pte. A. J. Moore

53648 10th. Btn Lancashire Fusiliers
Died September 18 1918, aged 28

Son of Robert & Sarah Ann Moore, Whittams Yard. Killed in action.

FONCQUEVILLERS MILITARY CEMETERY

Foncquevillers has 647 graves of Officers and Soldiers. 4 of these are German.

Lance Corporal Sam Barker

240422 6th Btn Sherwood Foresters
Died March 10 1917, aged 19

Son of the late Isaac & Annie Barker, Dig Street. Shown in Regimental Archives as a
grenadier. Killed in action by a bomb that fell short, the thrower being shot by the enemy.
This occurred when repelling an attack at Kite Copse.

GONNEHEIM BRITISH CEMETERY

Gonneheim contains 200 British Officers and Soldiers. It is approximately 4 miles/7km from Bethune.

Pte G. Mellor

53458 21st Btn West Yorkshire Regiment (Prince of Wales Own)
Died April 18 1918, aged 18

Son of late Henry & Harriet Mellor, Sturston.

GUARDS CEMETERY, LESBOEUFS

Guards Cemetery contains the graves of 3,136 Officers and Soldiers. 2,911 are British, 209 are Australian and 5 Canadian. At the time of the Armistice, the cemetery contained only 40 graves, mainly those of Grenadier Guards who died on September 25 1916. The cemetery was enlarged later when burials were brought in from the battlefields and smaller cemeteries in the area.

Pte W. T. Coxon

1623 53rd Btn Australian Infantry, A. I. F.
Died January 31 1917 aged 37

Son of the late William & Harriet Coxon, Hollands Yard, St John Street. He was cousin to Mr. W. Coxon (butcher), Victoria Square.

HARGICOURT BRITISH CEMETERY

Hargicourt British Cemetery contains the graves of 312 Officers and Soldiers, 273 are British. The cemetery is in the village of Aisne on the road to Peronne.

Pte. Mark Faulkner

203441 10th Btn Lincolnshire Regiment
Died August 26 1917,   aged 19

Son of John & Mary Faulkner, Old Derby Road. His body was taken out of the line and buried in the village (unspecified). Killed in action.

HAZEBROUCK COMMUNAL CEMETERY

Hazebrouck Communal Cemetery contains 878 war graves. This cemetery was close to a casualty clearing station. At first the casualties were buried amongst the civilian graves, but after the Armistice these burials were moved into the Commonwealth enclosure.

Pte Thomas Tunnicliffe

25485 18th Queen Mary's Own Hussars
Died May 22 1915, aged 26

Son of William Tunnicliffe, Union Street. Husband of Emmie Tunnicliffe née Ginnis, St. John Street. Father of James W. Tunnicliffe. Died of wounds.

KNIGHTSBRIDGE CEMETERY, MESNIL-MARTINSART

Knightsbridge cemetery contains the graves of 548 Officers and Soldiers, 400 are British. The cemetery, which is named after a communication trench which ran through the area, was begun at the outset of the Battle of the Somme, in 1916.

Corporal F. Moon

12992 10th Btn Cheshire Regiment
Died July 26 1916

Killed in action.

La FERTE-SOUS-JOUARRE MEMORIAL

La Ferte-Sous-Jouarre Memorial commemorates 3,740 Officers and Soldiers of the British Expeditionary Force who died in August, September and early October 1914. La Ferte-Sous-Jouarre is a small town 41miles/66km to the east of Paris. The memorial is situated in a small park on the banks of the River Marne.

THEY HAVE NO KNOWN GRAVE

Pte G. Skellern

9663 2nd Btn Sherwood Foresters
Died September 20 1914, aged 29

Son of Joseph & Elizabeth Skellern, Compton. Husband of Annie Skellern, Old Derby Road. Pte Skellern was the first Ashbourne man to die in the Great War. He was a regular soldier having served with the regiment for nine years, seven of these years were served in India. He was on reserve when War was declared and immediately recalled. One of the first to embark for France he was seconded to B Company 2nd Sherwood Foresters, 18th Brigade 6th Division. After taking part in one or two fierce engagements the regiment came under heavy fire on September 20th when he was killed. Later a letter to Mrs. Sowter, Old Derby Road from her son Fred states: "I am sorry to tell you a piece of bad news. We got into a terrible fight on Sunday with Germans and beat them, but am sorry to say that George Skellern got killed. I was with him but did not know he was dead until the fight was over." Before enlisting he worked for Messrs. Nestle and Anglo Condensed Milk Company at their Ashbourne factory where he was esteemed by his employers and workmates. He left a widow and two children, the last being born after the father left for France.

Mrs. Skellern subsequently remarried and her second husband Pte. S. Chell was also killed. This makes her the only woman in Ashbourne to lose two husbands to the war.

Le GRANDE HASARD MILITARY CEMETERY

Le Grande Hasard Military Cemetery contains 304 graves of the Great War. Of these 263 are British. It is in the village of Morbecque which lies 2miles/3km south west of Hazebrouck. The majority of the graves are from 1918.

Pte P. French

41730 11th Btn East Yorkshire Regiment
Died August 18 1918   aged 19

Son of Mr. & Mrs. French, South Street. Brother of Lance Corporal F.T. French on the Tyne Cot Memorial.

Le TOURET MILITARY CEMETERY, RICHEBOURG-L'AVOUE

Le Touret Military cemetery has 915 war graves. The Le Touret memorial to the Missing within the cemetery includes 4 VCs including Pte Jacob Rivers of Derby.

Pte F. Wibberley

281341 Sherwood Foresters
Died July 10 1916 aged 18

Son of Mr. & Mrs. Joseph Wibberley, St John Street. Killed in action by enemy shellfire when serving in the line at Ferme de Bois.

LOOS MEMORIAL

Loos Memorial commemorates 20,596 Officers and Soldiers with no known graves who fell in the area from the River Lys to the old Southern boundary of the 1st Army, east and west of Grenay.

Pte T.G. Carter

3541 1/6th Btn. Sherwood Foresters
Died October 15 1915 aged 19
    Son of Edward & Martha Carter, Market Place. Twin brother of Pte Charles Carter remembered on Menin Gate. Killed in action when the battalion was holding the Hohenzollern Redoubt.

Pte T.G. Carter

Pte Neville Massey

20047 2nd Btn Highland Light Infantry
Died October 2 1915 aged 21

Son of the late Joseph & Emma Massey.

MERVILLE COMMUNAL CEMETERY

Merville Communal Cemetery has British and Commonwealth graves, there are also 21
French and German.

Company Sergeant Major John Bradshaw

22801 15th Btn Royal Welsh Fusiliers
Died May 9 1916 aged 40

Son of John & Margaret Bradshaw of Stanton,
Ashbourne. Husband of Emma Bradshaw
Church Lane, Upper Mayfield.

He served through the South African War. He
was in many engagements and awarded many
medals and clasps. Giving up a good position
in January 1915 and rejoining the Colours, he
rapidly got promotion, ultimately attaining his
final position. On his death his Colonel described
him as "A Warrant Officer of the very best type,
a particularly brave man, and a thoroughly
good soldier." He received his wounds when
trying to help a wounded man, and for this act
of bravery his name was recommended for an
award before his wounds proved fatal. He left a
widow and 2 children, the youngest being four
months old who was never seen by its father.
He did leave behind several letters and diaries.
A diary that he kept during his voyage to South
Africa in 1896 is of great interest, telling of the
feelings of the soldiers on board. One poignant
entry tells of the death of a small child in the
night, her father being a Medical Officer on
board. She was buried at sea that afternoon, the
ensign being raised at half-mast.

Embarking from Malta in July 1896 he tells
of the excitement felt by the men at being on
board ship. At 5.00pm they all went on deck
to see Malta for the last time, as they steamed
out of harbour. There was cheering from the

The medal issued to all of the British combatants,
known as the 'Death Penny'

Maltese on shore wishing them well and a safe journey. The Lincolnshire Regt. and the Highland Light Infantry lined the quay as they left. He wrote of passing Tenerife and seeing the mountains for the first time and preparing to cross the Equator and meeting Neptune. He describes his first sight of African natives in canoes, "They have very flat noses and woolly hair with copper coloured skin." Very non-PC nowadays.

Diary extracts reads:

"Xmas Day 1915: in trenches, Germans fraternised with our troops for 15 minutes.
January 9 1916: 'A' company's billet shelled; rifle broken, 3 killed and injured.
April 20 1916: 2 patrols per night as far as German wire. 1 Nco, 2 men."

OVILLERS MILITARY CEMETERY, SOMME

Ovillers Military Cemetery contains of 3,559 graves of Officers and Soldiers of the Great War, 3,268 of these are British. Ovillers is in the heart of the Somme Battlefields. The cemetery was increased after the Armistice when Commonwealth and French graves were brought in mainly from the battlefields of Pozieres, La Boiselle, Ovillers and Contalmaison.

Pte F. Colclough

21732 9th Btn. Sherwood Foresters
Died September 15 1916 ,aged 31

Killed in action when serving in the trenches South of Thiepval.

PARGNY BRITISH CEMETERY, SOMME

Pargny British Cemetery contains 631 British graves and 6 Canadians.

Pte. G. Chapman

43023 22nd Btn. Durham Light Infantry
Died March 26 1918, aged 40

Husband of Florence May Chapman, Old Hill.

PHILOSOPHE BRITISH CEMETERY, MAZINGARBE

Philosophe British Cemetery contains 2,000 war graves. Marzinarbe is on the Loos salient.

Lance Sergeant J. E. Stevenson

204604 1/6th Btn Sherwood Foresters
Died November 4 1917, aged 31 (right)

Son of Edward & Mary Stevenson, Smiths Yard, Union Street. Killed in action during a raid on the German trenches near Verquin. His body was brought back to our lines by comrades.

Pte G. Etherington

269748 1/7th Btn Sherwood Foresters
Died October 25 1917, aged 30

Son of William & Sarah Ann Etherington, Compton. Killed in action when serving in the trenches at Hill 70.

POZIERES MEMORIAL

Pozieres Memorial commemorates 14,648 Officers and Soldiers of the British and South African forces with no known grave who died on the Somme battlefields between March 21st and August 7th 1918. Most are from March and April.

Sergeant G.W. Bennett M.M.

16469 5 Coy. 166 Btn. Sherwood Foresters
Died April 16 1918, aged 22

Son of Harriet Ann Bennett, Sturston Road.
Enlisting in May 1915 in the Sherwood Foresters in the 16th Btn (Chatsworth Rifles) he did his training at Redmines Camp, Sheffield before going to France on March 6th 1916. As a Corporal he was awarded the Military Medal on the first day of the 3rd battle of Ypres in 1917. His MM citation reads "For gallantry and devotion to duty during the operations in the St. Julien Sector between August 2nd and 5th 1917 when he bombed and cleared a German dugout." *London Gazette* November 2nd 1917. He was promoted to Sergeant. He was reported 'missing in action' in April 1918, near Wytschaete in Belgium during the last German

offensive of the war. He was very popular with his comrades. Before joining he worked for Richard Cooper, Ashbourne. His brother Pte Harry Bennett of the R.A.M.C. enlisted in February 1915, served in France for two years and ended the war in Italy.

Bombardier R.H. Beresford

35504 A Battery 95th Bde. Royal Field Artillery
Died March 21 1918

Pte R. Ward

76286 22nd Btn Durham Light Infantry
Died April 26 1918, aged 18

Son of Thomas Edward & Mary Ward, Peter Street.

Captain A.F.N. Henstock M.C.

15th Btn. Sherwood Foresters
Died March 22 1918, aged 26

Son of Mr. Thomas and Mrs. Catherine Henstock, Church Street. He was an extremely gifted child and whilst attending the local Wesleyan school won a scholarship at the age of 10 to the local Grammar School. He was school Captain in 1908/10 at the time of the opening of the new school on the Green Road site in 1909. At 16, he sat his London Matriculation Certificate being one of only 87 out of 2,000 candidates nationally to pass 1st class that year. He later gained other scholarships to enable him to attend the University of Wales at Aberystwyth. Here he played First X1 football, cricket and hockey. He was a prominent member of the Students Union council. He graduated in 1913 with a B.A. degree in Maths with 1st class honours, (being the only student to achieve that distinction that year).

Teaching at Hastings at the outbreak of war in 1914 he enlisted as a Pte in the Welsh Fusiliers. Following a year's training he was commissioned as an officer (a rare distinction for a grammar school boy and a baker's son). He was seconded to the 15th Btn Sherwood Foresters with whom he went to France. He was mentioned in despatches on three occasions and was awarded the Military Cross for exceptional bravery and skill in repelling a major raid German raid at Epehy.

On March 24th 1918 his battalion reached Curlu on the River Somme after marching all night and were sent to the front line without rest. After taking and holding a part of the line until late afternoon his company was cut off and the rest of the battalion ordered to retire. Although seriously wounded in the head he continued to command the company until retirement, but died on the way to the rear.

QUARRY CEMETERY, MONTAUBAN

Quarry British Cemetery contains 672 British Graves and 68 Australian, New Zealand and South African graves.

Gunner W. Sellers

64129 121st Siege Battery. Royal Garrison Artillery
Died December 28 1916, aged 19

Son of the late Charles & Mary Sellers of South Street.

St. HILAIRE CEMETERY, FREVENT,

St. Hilaire contains 210 Allied graves, 195 of these are British. Frevent was a place of some importance during the Great War on the lines of communication. The vast number of burials are from the number of Casualty Clearing Stations based here throughout the War. During World War II the greater part of Frevent was destroyed by bombing. An aerial torpedo fell in this cemetery, which is near the railway line, damaging the graves but the Commonwealth plot was not affected.

Gunner N. Walker

140514 B Battery 110th Brigade, Royal Field Artillery
Died March 27 1918

St SEVER CEMETERY, ROUEN

St. Sever cemetery contains 3,083 Commonwealth graves. During the Great War, Commonwealth camps and hospitals were based on the boundaries of Rouen. It is estimated that at least 18 hospitals were based here for the majority of the war.

2nd. Lt. Francis St. Vincent Morris

3rd. Squadron Royal Flying Corps.
3rd. Btn. Sherwood Foresters
Died April 29 1917, aged 21

Son of Canon Ernest E. Morris, M.A., T.D., J.P. & Josephine Morris of the Vicarage, Ashbourne. Born at Blackwell Vicarage he came to Ashbourne at the age of two and spent the early years here. He went to school at Bowden House, Harrow and subsequently transferred to Seaford. From there he entered Chichester House, Brighton College, in September 1910. He left Brighton in 1915 and was entered in the books of Wadham College, Oxford. He could not take up his place until after the war and on August 7th. was gazetted Second lieutenant in the Sherwood Foresters, where his father had been Chaplain for 18 years. Finding that his chances of getting across to France seemed remote, he transferred to the Royal Flying Corps. It was now that he got his only glimpse of Oxford, being quartered in Queen's College for four weeks whilst under instruction.

In the Spring of 1917 he crossed to France. On April 10th his machine was brought down by a blizzard at Vimy Ridge. His right leg and left thigh were fractured, and he received several cuts to his head. His right leg and foot had to be amputated and for a while he seemed to be making good progress. But another operation became imperative, and on Sunday April 29th he died peacefully under the anaesthetic at No. 2 General Hospital, Rouen. He was to have studied English and the Classics at Oxford and this probably accounts for the fact that now, along with Owen and Sassoon, he is a recognised War Poet. One of his most easily recognised is 'The Eleventh Hour' written in 1915.

The Eleventh Hour

Is this to love? - to cower and stand aside
While others fight and perish day by day?
To see my loved ones slaughtered and to say:
"Bravo! bravo! how nobly you have died!"

Is this to love? - to heed my friends no more,
But watch them perish in a foreign land
Unheeded, and to give no helping hand.
But smile, and say - "How terrible is war!"

Nay; this is not to love not this to live!
I will go forth; I hold no more aloof;
And I will give all that I have to give
And leave the refuge of my father's roof.

Then, if I live, no man will say, think I,
"He lives; because he did not dare to die."

Many years ago I was given a book that his mother had printed after his death and I would advise anyone interested in the poetry of this time to try to get a copy. It is one of my most treasured possessions.

TEMPLEUX-LE-GEURARD BRITISH CEMETERY,

Templeux-Le-Geurard cemetery contains the graves of 773 Officers and Soldiers.

Corporal J. G. Lowndes

240595 2/6th Btn. Sherwood Foresters
Died April 27 1917, aged 20

Son of Mr. John Thomas & Mrs. Georgina Lowndes, Buxton Road. Killed in action in the attack on the Quarries and Colagne Farm near Harcourt, France.

THIEPVAL MEMORIAL

Thiepval is a legendary site for all the nations of the former British Empire, which experienced its greatest tragedy here. Every year thousands of people cross the Channel to remember, during a unique and solemn ceremony. The Memorial was designed by Sir Edwin Lutyens and is immense and imposing. It bears the names of 73,367 soldiers who died and whose bodies have never been identified. It was opened 31 July 1932 by the Prince of Wales.

Thiepval Memorial

THE SOMME JULY 1st 1916

There can be few dates that capture the imagination like July 1 1916. It was when swathes of Kitcheners volunteer army left their trenches and strolled to their deaths on the first day of the battle of the Somme. After an eight day barrage of artillery and deep mine detonation beneath German strongholds, the first khaki-clad waves walked across no-man's land in the bright sunshine. Some of the volunteer soldiers even kicked footballs – after all they thought that none of the enemy could have survived the onslaught. The end of the first day saw 60,000 British casualties, but the fighting was to continue for months until November, with over 1.5 million casualties.

2nd Lt. Donald Callow

1/5th Btn. Sherwood Foresters Formerly of 1/4th Btn. London Regiment (London Scottish)
    Died July 1 1916, aged 19

  Son of Mr. J.M. & Mrs. Callow of Green Road, Ashbourne. He was educated at Ashbourne Queen Elizabeth's Grammar School and was expected to continue his education and train in Law. He was wounded in October 1914 and returned to the front later.

2nd. Lt. S.W. Moult

2nd. Btn. Sherwood Foresters
Died September 15 1916, aged 28

  Son of Thomas & Emma Moult. He served in the 17th Lancers and was at the Curragh Barracks in Ireland with the 2nd Lt. 4th Btn. Sherwood Foresters May 6th 1915. He joined 2nd Btn. June 6th 1916 at Canal Bank. Killed in action September 15th 1916 at Arrowhead Copse, Guillemont.

Pte J. Braddock

3447 1/4th Btn Northumberland Fusiliers
Died September 15 1916

Pte. W. Le-Grice

22800 18th Btn. Lancashire Fusiliers
Died April 15 1917

  Son of Mr. & Mrs. W. Le-Grice, Durham Ox, Compton. Born in Ashbourne after his parents came from Burton on Trent to take over the Durham Ox Inn. He married and left two children, a son Colin and a daughter Hazel.

Pte P. Sharpe MM

12244 2nd. Btn. Sherwood Foresters
Died September 16 1916

Son of Sgt. E. Sharpe (Derbyshire Constabulary) & Mrs. Sharpe of the Lock-Up, Belle Vue Road. Killed in action in the trenches near Guillemont, France.

Pte H. Slater

17355 C. Comp. 10th Btn Sherwood Foresters
Died July 7 1916, aged 23

Son of Mr. & Mrs. William Slater, 91 Mayfield Road. Went to France in June 1915, was wounded February 1916 and returned to England for treatment. Was killed in action in the attack on the Quadrangle Support near Contalmaison, France. He was the brother of Gdsm. O.E. Slater RVM named on the Menin Gate. This was the second son of Mr. and Mrs. Slater to have no known grave.

Pte A. Adair Thompson

28074 1st. Btn East Surrey Regiment
Died September 3 1916 aged 23
Son of Robert & Elizabeth Thompson, 41 Church Street. Husband of Mary Philomena Thompson, 41 Church Street. The family were greengrocers and florists (later H. Sweeney).

VIS-EN-ARTOIS MEMORIAL

Vis-en-Artois memorial commemorates 9,822 Officers and Soldiers with no known grave who fell in the period between August 8 1916 to the date of Armistice, in the advance to Victory in Picardy and Artois, between the Somme and Loos.

Pte J. Grimes

91730 1/6th Btn. Sherwood Foresters
Died September 29 1918 aged 23

Son of Mr. & Mrs. Samuel Grimes, Buxton Road. Killed in the action near Lihaucourt, France.

Pte J. Moon

307079 8th. Btn. Sherwood Foresters
Died October 3 1918 aged 26

Son of J. Moon, Stag and Pheasant Yard, Compton. His grandfather was born in India whilst his father was serving in the British Army. Later his grandfather was to become a Chelsea Pensioner. 1t was very unusual to have a registered Pensioner living in the town. He was what is known as an 'Out-Lyer'. That is someone in receipt of a pension but living at home with his family. Killed in action when in the attack on Ramicourt and Montbrahain.

WARLINCOURT HALTE
BRITISH CEMETERY, SAULTY

Warlincourt Halte Cemetery contains 1,296 graves, 29 of them are German. It was used from June 1916 by Casualty Clearing Stations.

Pte Robert Spencer

4511 'C' Company 1/6th Sherwood Foresters
Died September 21 1916 aged 18

Son of Mr. & Mrs. J. F. Spencer 3 Hall Bank, Green Road. I have been extremely fortunate to have been given access to the family records and correspondence referring to Pte. Spencer's death. It is most unusual after such a long time and with the passing of generations to find a family that have so much knowledge. Pte. Spencer was the second of seven children, and he was one of those brave young men who were not completely truthful about their age when enlisting. He was only 18 when he died, but had been at war for over a year.

Records show that Pte. Spencer died of wounds following action in the village of Brules near Bellacourt. However, the family have a most interesting letter from the Surgeon that treated him. It is a long letter but I will quote some of the more interesting points, which give an insight into conditions in a Field Hospital:

"It is such a long time since it happened and we have had so many sick and wounded through our hands that I have nearly forgotten his last words ..... your son was admitted into my ward about 11.30. He was conscious but in much pain. He had a bullet wound in his left side close to the hip. The bullet passed through the lower intestines, and we found it later. It had also pierced his bladder. We knew that the case was hopeless. An operation was performed at once ..... it was a long job. The surgeons managed to abstract the bullet which I saw and put it in the little bag with his belongings. It was a machine gun bullet which was then a new type, slightly smaller than an English bullet with a very sharp point .... the lad was conscious for intervals during the night. He was not in great pain for he had large injections to deaden it. He spoke in most affectionate terms of his parents, he gave me their address and begged me to say 'goodbye'.

He spoke of some young lady – I forget if it was his sister or sweetheart ..... he passed away peacefully about breakfast time. He had every care and it is little comfort to say that he died in bed free from pain. When a patient comes into a C.C.S. (Casualty Clearing Station) and we know that there is little chance of recovery we make straight for his pockets to find his identification disc and particulars. In his

pocket I found a pocket book containing an old photograph and two letters along with a birthday card from his mother. I took off him a common wristwatch and they were all put together in a little linen bag such as we keep for such occasions. His effects would be sent to the ordnance depot for despatch home ..... I am always in need of something for my poor boys and no doubt if your premises were near here I could find tons of useful stuff, in fact I would willingly burgle it at the first opportunity. It would not be the first time I have pinched stuff for them since I have been in France. Maybe I should say 'commandeered'. I might say that in these places cigarettes are always more than welcome, today I don't have one in the place."

A short part of a long letter which describes some harrowing details, which I think are better not recalled.

EGYPT

ISMAILA WAR MEMORIAL CEMETERY

Ismailia War Memorial Cemetery contains 372 graves from the Great War. There are 291 World War II burials. The cemetery also contains 297 non-war graves. Ismailia is a small town on the west-side of the Suez canal. The cemetery was started in 1915 following an unsuccessful attack by Turkish forces.

Pte. Joseph Salt

51180 2nd. Btn. Imperial Camel Corps.
Died August 26 1918

A man born in Ashbourne and living in the town at the time of his death, however, I can find no Army records and he may have been related to Cpl. R. H. Salt, son of Israel Salt, Mayfield Road.

GIBRALTAR

GIBRALTAR (NORTH FRONT) CEMETERY

Gibraltar North Front Cemetery is also known as the Garrison Cemetery. This cemetery was used during the Great War for the burial of Sailors and Soldiers who died on the ships passing Gibraltar, or in the Military Hospital. The cemetery also contains Australian and New Zealand men from Gallipoli who died on ships on the way back to Britain. There are 692 burials.

Pte. W. Foxon

55303 28th Coy. Royal Army Medical Corps.
Died October 30 1918 aged 25

Son of Frederick & Elizabeth Foxon, 40 Mayfield Road.

GREECE

MIKRA BRITISH CEMETERY, KALAMARIA, GREECE

Mikra British Cemetery has 1,810 burials of the Great War. Within the cemetery can be found the Mikra Memorial commemorating 500 nurses, officers and men of the Commonwealth forces who died when Troop Transport and Hospital Ships were lost in the Mediterranean, and who have no known grave but the sea.

Pioneer H. Wright

191588 4th. Air Line Section, Royal Engineers
Died January 4 1919 aged 33

Husband of Annie Wright, 87 Mayfield Road.

IRAQ

BBC NEWS

Lost British graveyard found in Iraq

The Royal British Legion has welcomed news that a lost graveyard for World War I dead has been found in central Iraq. The cemetery at Al Amara, built for those on the Mesopotamian Expeditionary Force, has been discovered by the banks of the Tigris River. It was found by the Royal Irish Regiment, who on Easter Sunday will say prayers at the cemetery for those who died and for the current armed forces. The site had been protected by its Iraqi keeper, who received death threats from Baath officials.

Hassan Hatif Moson, a 40-year-old father of seven, told the *Daily Mail*, in a pooled despatch from Iraq:

"The old regime, they threatened my life and my job but I never gave up. I could not permit the graveyard to be ruined – local people have tried to break in here to drink late at night and also to steal the carvings. I always believed that one day the British would return."

Good news

The cemetery, which includes two Victoria Cross winners, was abandoned by the Commonwealth War Graves Commission after the last Gulf War. Jeremy Lillies, head of public affairs for the Royal British Legion, said:

"This is very good news. It is extremely good to hear that this chap has stuck to his guns in the face of a great deal of intimidation to keep the place in as good order as he could do. The good news now is that something can be done about it."

He said the Commonwealth War Graves Commission had a warehouse full of new headstones in Baghdad, but their distribution had been delayed by the war.

The headstones at Al Amara were plundered by an earlier Iraqi regime in 1937. But Mr. Hassan kept the memorial polished, saved the masonry from looters and cut the grass. He worked without pay since the last Gulf War and kept all the documents relating to the graveyard since he took the keeper's job in 1977. That thoughtfulness will enable thousands of British families to trace the final resting place of their loved ones.

Royal Irish Commanding Officer, Lt Colonel Tim Collins, led a team of officers in search of the cemetery after hearing about it from local people. He said:

"It is quite remarkable what Mr. Hassan has achieved – this place has been better tended than some of the war graves in France. He has shown great respect to the British and courage in the face of the Baath regime by carrying this burden of the empire."

The two Victoria Cross recipients are Royal Naval Lt Commander Edgar Cookson and Lt Colonel Edward Henderson of the North Staffordshire Regiment.

The condition of Al Amara was in contrast with another British military cemetery near Basra, which was found in a state of disrepair. It contained hundreds of soldiers and officials who died over a series of campaigns from 1880 onwards.

THEY ARE NOT LOST THEY, THEY ARE HERE

[Story from BBC NEWS:
http://news.bbc.co.uk/go/pr/fr/-/1/hi/world/middle__east/2958143.stm

Published: 2003/04/18 06:31:44 GMT

© BBC MMVIII]

Pte. R. H. Everatt

16146 2nd Btn. Leicestershire Regt.
Died November 11 1916

Little is known of him except that he was buried in the lost cemetery of Almara on the Turkish/Iraq border.

BASRA MEMORIAL

The Basra Memorial commemorates 40,654 Commonwealth Officers and Soldiers with no known grave who died in operations in Mesopotamia between Autumn 1914 and August 1921. The Memorial was located in the dockyard at Maqil 5 miles/8 kilometres from Basra until 1997. President Sadaam Hussein was so incensed by the British following the 1st Gulf War that he decreed that it should be moved as far as possible into the desert. It was moved 20miles/32 kilometres and no one was allowed to visit it. In 2008 it was retaken by British Forces and can now be seen again in its full glory.

Captain Francis John Rigby MC

3rd. Btn. Seaforth Highlanders
Died January 21 1916, aged 27

Son of John Richard & Clara Rigby, St. John Street.

Pte. Rowland Harding

23257 6th. Btn. King's Own (Royal Lancaster Regt.)
Died February 9 1917, aged 25

Son of James & Alice Harding, Compton. He was the second son of Mr. and Mrs. Harding to die in the Great War. Joined the Sherwood Foresters 3rd. Btn April 22nd 1916 and was transferred to Lancaster Regt. on May 5th 1916. Killed in action.

ISRAEL

JERUSALEM MEMORIAL, ISRAEL

The Jerusalem Memorial commemorates 3,296 Commonwealth Officers and Soldiers with no known grave who died in operations in Egypt and Palestine. It is situated in Jerusalem War Cemetery.

Pte. Bert Westhorpe

201476 1/5th. Btn Royal Scots Fusiliers
Died April 19 1917, aged 22

Son of John & Emma Westhorpe, 114 Mayfield Road.

ITALY

MONTECCHIO PRECALEINO COMMUNAL CEMETERY

Montecchio Precaleino Communal Cemetery Extension is in the Vicenza province. It contains 439 Commonwealth burials of the Great War. Italy entered the War on the Allied side after declaring war on Austria in May 1915. Commonwealth forces were on the Italian Front from November 1917 to November 1918. Between April 1918 and February 1919 those who died from wounds or disease at the Casualty Clearing Stations were buried either here or at Dueville.

Corp. James Milward

825338 'B' Battery 24th Brigade Royal Field Artillery
Died January 5 1919, aged 36

Son of William and Jane Milward

MALTA

CAPUCCINI NAVAL CEMETERY

Malta Naval Cemetery contains 2,625 World War I and World War II casualties. It contains service men of all the Armed Services. This includes 22 men who died when *H.M.S. Russell* was sunk by a mine off Malta in April 1916. It is divided into Roman Catholic and Protestant plots. The earth is shallow on Malta and during both wars many joint or collective burials were made as graves had to be cut in underlying rock.

Midshipman G.P.C. Wetherall

H.M.S. Russell, Royal Navy
Died April 27 1916

PIETA MILITARY CEMETERY, MALTA

Pieta Military Cemetery contains 1,303 graves of Officers and Soldiers from the Great War. World War II burials number 166. From early 1915 the hospitals and convalescent depots on the islands of Malta and Gozo dealt with over 135,000 sick and wounded, chiefly from the campaigns in Gallipoli and Salonika. Increased submarine activity in the Mediterranean meant that fewer hospital ships were sent to the islands from May 1917.

Sapper Harry Kitchen

64736 13th Signal Comp. Royal Engineers
Died September 2 1915 aged 22

Son of Thomas & Rose Annie Kitchen of Ashbourne.
Sapper Kitchen's brother, Clifford, of the Sherwood Foresters was killed outside Ypres in October 1918.

TURKEY

HELLES MEMORIAL, TURKEY

Helles Memorial stands on the tip of the Gallipoli Peninsula. It takes the form of an obelisk over 98ft/30m high that can be seen by ships passing through the Dardanelles. The number of identified casualties is 20,835 with no known grave, though the actual figure is thought to be much higher.

Pte. Joseph Barnes

1602 Derbyshire Yeomanry
Died August 21 1915,   aged 24

Son of Joseph & Ellen Barnes, Victoria Square. Killed in action.

Pte. George Hill

10690 6th Btn. Lancashire Regiment
Died August 1915

Pte. George Henry Hudson

17824 9th Btn. Sherwood Foresters
Died September 22 1915

Son of Mr. & Mrs. T. Hudson, Union Street. Killed in action in Gallipoli.

UNITED KINGDOM

ASHBOURNE CEMETERY, MAYFIELD ROAD

Ashbourne Cemetery contains seven Great War Graves and seventeen World War II.

Colour Sergeant Frederick Bull

2900 6th Reserve Btn. Sherwood Foresters
Died November 23 1914, aged 42

Husband of Elizabeth Bull, Hall Flats, Ashbourne. Died of illness contracted on service.

Pte. F. Chell

203514 lst Btn. Sherwood Foresters
Died November 13 1918, aged 26

Husband of Emma Chell, Station Street. Served with the Territorials but had left before the War, being placed on Reserve. Recalled, and landed in France February 28th 1915. He was with 'C' Company and wounded at Zillebeke July 12th 1915. 1n 1916 he had been recalled to serve in the Irish Rebellion before going again to France, where he was badly gassed and returned home. He died at home from gas wounds.

Pte. S. Chell

10809 3rd Btn. Sherwood Foresters
Died January 3 1918

Son of Mr. Edward Chell, Compton and husband of Annie Chell (previously Skellern), 25 Old Derby Road.

Enlisted at Normanton Barracks in 1904, and was at the Barracks when War was declared. Served in France and was wounded by a bullet in the right hand. He was discharged from the Army, as no longer fit for service in 1915 after taking part in the battle of Aisne. He had a full Military funeral in Ashbourne. He was the second husband of Annie to die as a result of the War.

Pte. W. Fearn

71086 2nd Btn. Sherwood Foresters
Died May 10 1919, aged 29

Son of Harry Fearn. Enlisted 1914 and was gassed 1919. Goaled the Ashbourne Shrovetide Football 1918 whilst home on leave. He died in Ashbourne Cottage Hospital as a result of gassing.

Pte. Edward Wibberley

23310 6th Btn. Kings Own (Royal Lancashire Regiment)
Died January 30 1918, aged 32

Husband of Cecily Wibberley, née Harlow. Served with the Territorials prior to the outbreak of War and then with the 3rd Btn. Sherwood Foresters L Company until April 22nd 1916. Was transferred to 3rd Btn. Royal Lancaster Regiment May 5th 1916 then sent to Mesopotamia where he was wounded and discharged as unfit for further service in November 1916. Died of complications from his wounds at Ashbourne Cottage Hospital.

Pte. William Wyche

M/300590 M.T. Army Service Corps
Died August 11 1918, aged 19

Pte. F.W. Bates

80911 1/8th Btn. Durham Light Infantry
Died September 11 1919, aged 19

Son of Frederick and Elizabeth Bates (Bakers), Compton

He was posted to Rugeley in 1917 before being sent to France in April 1918. He was at the battle of Lawe and Lys in the area of Bethune on April 17th. Part of the 151st

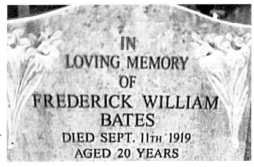

Infantry Brigade, consisting of 162 newly trained men, mostly 19 year olds, were sent as reinforcements. They fought and lost their first battle. Three days later after training, 648 men of all ranks moved by train to NEUF (North European United Forces) Berquin. At 0-100 hours (?1am) on April 9th they were under orders to relieve a Portuguese Unit in the line. Three hours later the Germans launched a massive attack and the Portuguese retreated. The result was that the 151st Brigade position became the front line. Between April 9-14th the 1/8th Btn. were involved in continuous fighting with constant bombardment and a series of attacks. They held the line at the River Lawe.

Pte. Bates was seriously wounded. His record reads: "Gunshot to right chest. Bullet entered penetrating right side below clavicle, through to cervical spine and lodged beneath the scapula. Unfit for service and granted a pension for 12 months. Marked collapse of the chest wall resulting in Emphysema. 70% disablement." He was discharged in January 1919 and returned home. He died as a result of wounds in September 1919. His family gave to St. John's Church a silver Altar Cross in his memory. The inscription around the base reads: "In loving memory of Frederick William Bates. Died September 11 1919 as a result of the Great War."

ST. OSWALD'S CHURCHYARD, MAYFIELD ROAD

St. Oswald's contains 2 Great War graves and one World War I casualty is buried here.

Pte. J. Lee

809 'D' Company Sherwood Foresters
Died March 11 1918, aged 34

Son of the late Mr. T. Lee & Mrs. Lee of Birches Terrace, Station Street. Joined 1st Btn. March 21st 1915 and served with 'A' Company. He was sent home suffering from shell shock and had been undergoing treatment at Derby County Mental Hospital since November 1915. He died there. This is the only case that I have come across with the death designated as "Death from shell shock."

Pte. H. Wibberley

162649 Gun Corps. (Infantry)

Son of Mrs. C. Wibberley, Derby Road. I can find no reference to his wounds or illness, but I assume that he suffered and died at home.

ST. OSWALD'S PARISH CHURCH, ASHBOURNE

A brass plaque on the west wall of the Church commemorates a man killed near Ypres.

2nd. Lt. Bernard Gibbs MC

6th attached 1st Btn. Rifle Brigade (The Prince Consort's Own)
Died July 7 1915

Youngest son of G.R. Gibbs & Elizabeth, née Wise, of Ashbourne. Gazetted. "For the cool and capable way in which he commanded the Canadian Dressing Station and outbuildings while the Germans sapped to within 40 yards of it. He opened enfilade fire on a considerable force attacking his left bringing them to a standstill. Later he ran into the open and threw hand grenades at the German sapping party, compelling them to retire." Killed in the action.

NORWICH CEMETERY, NORFOLK

Cpl. William Sawers

15383 2nd Station Hospital Royal Army Medical Corps
Died July 13 1915, aged 35

Husband of Ethel May Sawers, Station Street, Ashbourne. No cause of death recorded. Memorial plaque in St. John's Church, Buxton Road.

PLYMOUTH NAVAL MEMORIAL

Plymouth Naval Memorial commemorates 23,185 men of the Royal Navy including over 15,000 men from World War II. After the Great War an appropriate way of remembering those members of the Royal Navy who had no known grave was sought, the majority of deaths having occurred at sea where no permanent memorial could be provided. An Admiralty committee recommended that the three manning ports of Great Britain – Chatham, Plymouth and Portsmouth – should have an identical memorial of unmistakeable naval form, an obelisk, which would serve as a leading mark for shipping.

Midshipman Denzil Charles Tudball

H.M.S. Indefatigable, Royal Navy
Died May 31 1916

Opposite: The Plymouth Naval Memorial, with Drake in the foreground. The Hoe, Plymouth
Previous page: The memorial to Bernasrd Gibbs is the one on the far left

SOME LESSER KNOWN FACTS

Ashbourne has a unique place in the memorials to the Great War.

What is now the Ashbourne Royal British Legion was originally known as The Ashbourne Comrades Club and became affiliated after 1921. When the Standard was dedicated on October 18 1931 it was the occasion on which Ashbourne entered the record books. A grand parade and service of dedication was organised and the whole town took part. It started in the Market Place where 250 ex-soldiers gathered along with dignitaries to parade to the Church. The streets were lined with people. The service was taken by the Vicar Canon L. Shaw who welcomed everyone. The service of dedication was to be led by Rt. Rev. Herbert Bury DD, Assistant Bishop of London and formerly Bishop for North and Central Europe during the War. He announced that he had a message for the people of Ashbourne from Viscount Plumer, President of the Ypres Memorial Settlement Committee, thanking them for the collection they made in 1924.

1t was the very first money raised for the Memorial to be known as the Menin Gate. The message also said:

"We thought of a Church only, but now we have also a Parsonage, School and Hostel and by special legislation of the Belgian Government our settlement is now forever British territory. Ashbourne gave us the first subscription in the country." Another unique way of connecting the Ypres Memorial Church with Ashbourne was adopted when the Ashbourne Branch presented the Memorial Church with handsomely bound copies of the Bible Prayer book and Hymn book for the Bishop's Chair. Each book is neatly inscribed "For the Bishop's Chair in the Ypres Memorial Church" given by the Ashbourne Branch of the British Legion on October 18 1931.

The Standard was given by Mrs. Peveril-Turnbull of Sandybrook Hall.

COMMONWEALTH WAR GRAVES COMMISSION

Too old to be accepted for army duty, Fabian Ware arrived in France in command of a mobile unit of the British Red Cross in September 1914. He was struck by the lack of organisation responsible for the marking of the graves of the fallen soldiers and became determined that this should change. With his persistence the War Office realised that the proper care of war graves would boost the morale of troops at the front and comfort relatives at home. The work that Ware had started of recording and maintaining graves was recognised and the foundation of the Graves Registration Commission in 1915 became part of the army. As early as 1916 Ware encouraged help from horticulturists from Kew and the most eminent architects of the day on how the cemeteries and memorials should be designed.

On 21 May 1917 his diligence was recognised when the Imperial (now Commonwealth) War Graves Commission was established by Royal Charter. During the war Fabian Ware was twice mentioned in despatches and ended the war as a Major-General. In 1920 he became a Knight of two orders in recognition of his tireless work during the Great War. Major-General Sir Fabian Ware died on 28 April 1949 and is buried in the Churchyard in Amberley where his grave is marked by a Commission headstone.

It was decided that the grave yards should not look like ordinary cemeteries and that they should not be laid out by Rank as all were equal, and that they should look like

English gardens. Mrs. Jaeckels was consulted as was Sir Edwin Lutyens who had had previous experience in commemorative architecture. He designed the Sword of Sacrifice which is to be seen in all War Graves cemeteries no matter how small. Mrs. Jaeckels advised on the planting and Rudyard Kipling (who had lost his son Jack in the war) composed the epitaphs.

LABOUR BATTALIONS

Labour Battalions perhaps have not received the recognition due to them. Especially in the Great War they were a very necessary part of the Army. Mainly made up of men too old to serve as soldiers, they did their bit. Our area provided men who had special skills such as quarrying and coal mining which were important in building and maintaining trenches. They undertook road mending and trench reinforcements Tasks which were not glorious or medal gaining but essential to the War effort.

SOME OTHER NEWS FROM
ASHBOURNE AND DISTRICT
Extracts from the Ashbourne Telegraph June 29 1917

Cpt. R.H. Bond of the Derbyshire Territorials has been promoted to the rank of Adjutant. He was attached to General Stuart-Wortley's staff in France. He was mentioned in despatches for exceptional work on the staff.

Lieut. L. Taylor of the Manchester Regiment has been gazetted to the rank of Captain. Captain Taylor is the son of Nurse Taylor of Park Road. He responded to his Country's call in 1914 as a Pte. in the "PALS" Manchester Regiment. Promotion followed swiftly and he was gazetted Lieutenant in October 1915.

Cadet Probert-Jones has been granted a Commission in the Manchester Regiment. 2nd. Lt. Jones has seen several months of service in France and was present at the memorable battle of Delville Wood. The latter was one of the bloodiest battles of the Somme, including men of the 1st South African Regiment. Despite losing 80% of its men, it held until relieved and is now the home of the South African Memorial, a replica of their Parliament Building.

Sapper W. Thornley was promoted to the rank of Sergeant in the Telegraphic Section of the Royal Engineers. After serving in France for 2 years, Sgt. Thornley was mentioned, for special services, in Sir Douglas Haig's despatches.

Corporal F. Cheadle R.E. the eldest of 6 sons who are all serving. Son of Mr.& Mrs. J. Cheadle, South Street he has been promoted to the rank of Sergeant. Formerly an employee of the L and NW Railway he has served 2 years in France.

Sgt. T. Eaton was in the 6th. Btn. Sherwood Foresters when War was declared had held a good position at R. Cooper & Co. His clerical abilities attracted attention both at Camp and Headquarters. The Btn. moved, but Sgt. Eaton was retained at Chesterfield in recruiting and running of Headquarters. Sgt. Eaton's only regret is that he was separated from his comrades.

Corporal C.W. Wood for a few years Corporal Wood was engaged by the *Derbyshire Advertiser*, but at the outbreak of war he was working for Cull, Brett and Osborne, Solicitors. He had several narrow escapes whilst in the field, and was only a short distance from the eight brave Ashbourne boys who lost their lives together in the trench where they were billeted resulting from a direct hit by a German shell. He is one of the few Territorials who was neither ill nor wounded after leaving England. He was lucky.

Company Sgt. Major George Dakin MM of the 1/6th Btn. Sherwood Foresters. He was the first Ashbourne man to be awarded the MM. He landed in France February 28th 1915 and was awarded his MM on November 11th 1916. He was with 'B' Company and was wounded at Fonquillers on January 11th 1917. He returned to duty and was again wounded July 1st 1917 at Cite St. Pieffe. He was sent to hospital in Sheffield. He was discharged from service May 4th 1919.

Lance Corporal S. Gilman MM was born in Ashbourne but lived later in Alstonefield. He was killed during the attack on the lines at Mory Vabbaye, France. He has no known grave and is on the Arras Memorial. His citation reads "For gallantry and devotion to duty during operations at Jeancourt on March 31st 1917 when the battalion successfully attacked and captured the villages of Vendelles and Jeancourt."

Pte. W. Birch of Mayfield is another member of the Ashbourne Territorials who was in the trench with the three Ashbourne soldiers – Lance Corp. Albert Harrison, Pte. Fred Bull and Pte. Walter Blake – who were killed by a German high explosive shell. Pte. Birch escaped a similar fate but received a wound in the head from a fragment of the same shell. He received treatment but was returned to England afterwards.

Lance Corporal S. Gilman MM

Pte. W. Birch

PRISONERS OF WAR

As at the time of the Napoleonic Wars, Ashbourne was again responsible for Prisoners of War. It is said that Officers were billeted at Ashbourne Hall, but I have found no mention of 'other ranks'. However, I have found a certificate of prisoners being held in a camp. I do not know where! Like the French prisoners it would appear that they had to work for their living.

P. of War Camp, Ashbourne.

Army Book 57.

Station_____ Date___ 31/1/ 19/9

RECEIVED of* *Mr. A. Garland and R. Garland.*
for the late. J. Garland.

the sum of *Nineteen shillings and three pence*

in respect of *Work done by Prisoners of War.*

£ —: 19: 3.

Hamblay Commandant

'Insert the designation of the
P. of War Officer making the payment.' *ne.*

A LETTER FROM THE TRENCHES

I make no apologies for my final entry. I feel proud that although **Sgt. H. Wright** is not essentially an Ashbourne man he should be recorded. Born of a Fenny Bentley family he would have been well known in the town and as such deserves a mention. Our most decorated man of who, I had never heard, until descendants of the family contacted me. I also feel that to do his story justice I should reproduce his letter [see below] which gives us an insight into the life our men were living in the trenches. Harry Wright returned and eventually emigrated to Canada to begin a new life. His medals and honours are in the hands of his family who are proud of Granddad. For this man of humble origins to be honoured not only by his own Country but by France and Italy for outstanding bravery is to be remembered.

"We came out of the trenches the other day; my word, I was pleased. You see, our rifles get clogged, and the empty cases won't extract. I can't tell you what it feels like to have a rifle in your hand, and an empty case stuck in the breech that won't extract, and the order comes along "they (the Germans) are advancing," and you are stuck in a trench with a rifle that you can't fire a round with. I can tell you we get some queer thoughts in our heads at times. Fancy only 80 yards between our trenches and those of the Germans. But they hardly ever get to us, but if they do there is only a few of them, and of course you can imagine what happens; everyone of us with fixed bayonets, they don't get back to say how many of us there are.

One night we had a night march to a place, I dare not tell you the name of it; the Sherwoods were the advance guard to the brigade. We got there about 11pm and we found the bridge was blown up, leading into the place. The infantry got over, but we could not get any carts or guns over. As soon as we got there the Germans set the church on fire; they had poured petrol over it, and it lit the place up just like day. We took it at the bayonet point, and then had to search the houses. You never saw such an awful state of affairs in your life just fancy them coming to Ashbourne and turning everything in the houses into the streets – beds, furniture, and everything that people had left behind, which were thrown into the streets, and the front rooms turned into stables. It makes you thank God that England is surrounded by water. It is awful day after day, week after week, one continuous battle. But it can't last for ever and we shall win.

We have never had our clothes off since we left Cambridge; we get a new article now and then and put that on and throw the other away…Remember me to all the people in Bentley, and, I hope dear mother and dad, that we shall all be spared to unite once more in the old home and then we will have a good rejoicing."

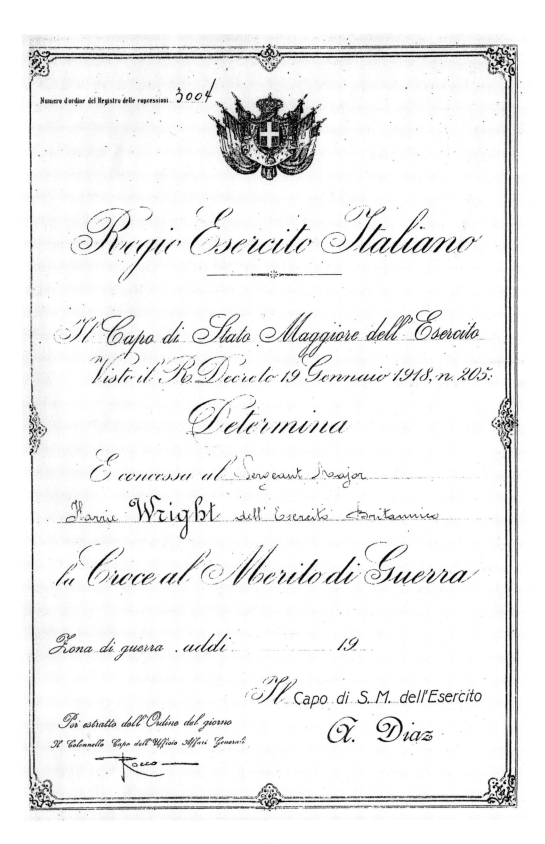

INDEX TO NAMES